NAMES AND RIVERS

Hyoryubutsu (Driftage)

Sekai—Kai (The World—The Sea)

Moboroshi-no-Haha (The Illusory Mother)

Chikyu-Sosei-Setsu (One Genesis of the World)

Sen-no-Namae (A Thousand Names—Mille Nomina)

Iteki—Barbaroi (Barbarians)

Kido Shuri Shishu (The Selected Poems of Shuri Kido)

Man'bo (Manbo—Sunfish)

Kozukata-Sho (Some Thoughts on Kozukata)

Hitetsu (Nonferrous)

Monsun-Kikotai (Monsoon Climatic Zone)

Shokan (Shokan—Cited—Cité)

NAMES AND RIVERS

SELECTED POEMS BY SHURI KIDO

TRANSLATED BY TOMOYUKI ENDO AND FORREST GANDER

COPPER CANYON PRESS
PORT TOWNSEND, WASHINGTON

Cover photograph: Keiko Onoda, from *Water Series: Finland,* 2015

Copper Canyon Press is in residence at Fort Worden State Park in Port Townsend, Washington, under the auspices of Centrum. Centrum is a gathering place for artists and creative thinkers from around the world, students of all ages and backgrounds, and audiences seeking extraordinary cultural enrichment.

LIBRARY OF CONGRESS CATALOGING-IN-PUBLICATION DATA
Names: Kido, Shuri, 1959– author. | Endo, Tomoyuki, translator.
| Gander, Forrest, 1956– translator.
Title: Names and rivers : selected poems by Shuri Kido / Shuri Kido ;
translated by Tomoyuki Endo and Forrest Gander.
Description: Port Townsend, Washington : Copper Canyon Press, [2022]
| Parallel text in Japanese and English on facing pages.
| Summary: "A collection of poems by Shuri Kido, translated by Tomoyuki Endo and
Forrest Gander"— Provided by publisher.
Identifiers: LCCN 2022021806 (print) | LCCN 2022021807 (ebook)
| ISBN 9781556596612 (paperback) | ISBN 9781619322615 (epub)
Subjects: LCSH: Kido, Shuri, 1959– Translations into English.
| LCGFT: Poetry. Classification: LCC PL872.5.I33 N36 2022 (print)
| LCC PL872.5.I33 (ebook) | DDC 895.61/5—dc23/eng/20220506
LC record available at https://lccn.loc.gov/2022021806
LC ebook record available at https://lccn.loc.gov/2022021807

98765432 FIRST PRINTING

COPPER CANYON PRESS
Post Office Box 271
Port Townsend, Washington 98368
www.coppercanyonpress.org

ACKNOWLEDGMENTS

Thanks to the editors of the following journals where translations first appeared, some in different versions:

AGNI: "The Inertia of Anxiety" and "Kozukata (The Road Never to Be Taken)"

Harvard Review: "Alchemy of Summer," "The Portrayal of White," and "A Thousand Vowels"

Poetry: "The Dry Season" and "Wandering Beyond"

Poetry Daily: "A Thousand Vowels"

The St. Ann's Review: "The Portrayal of White" and "Toward Temple Risshaku"

Veritas Review: "The Direction North," "Nonferrous," and "Ritual Utensils"

World Literature Today: "Wandering Birds"

ZYZZYVA: "The Rejected Light" and "A Tiny Little Equation"

CONTENTS

My collaboration with the scholar-translator Tomoyuki Endo began years ago when we were asked to cotranslate some poems by the legendary contemporary poet Kazuko Shiraishi for a book published by New Directions. Endo is, among other things, a deeply knowledgeable and bilingual enthusiast of modernist and contemporary poetry in English and Japanese. By that time, I had already cotranslated, with Kyoko Yoshida, *Spectacle & Pigsty,* a book of poems by Kiwao Nomura (which won Three Percent/University of Rochester's Best Translated Book Award), and later I'd edited a wild, sui generis book, *Alice Iris Red Horse,* by the writer/artist Gozo Yoshimasu. It was Yoshimasu, at a party in his apartment in Tokyo, who introduced me to the poet Shuri Kido and to Kido's wife, the well-regarded photographer Keiko Onoda. That night, Kido gifted me with two of his books.

A few years later, when I was in Japan with Ashwini Bhat, Shuri and Keiko invited us to dinner with Tomoyuki (Tom), and we all talked about the possibility of translating a book of Kido's poetry. Tom was game to give it a try, and so was I. Our earlier work together— with Shiraishi—had gone well and been a pleasure for me.

So Shuri Kido put together a small selection of poems. Tom went through Shuri's various books and added other poems that he thought were strong and might translate well. And we started with those, chronologically. We worked on the poems for more than two years. Tom initiated the process with first drafts and light glosses. I asked endless questions, many of which only Shuri himself could answer. Some were concerned with Buddhism and language philosophy, some with syntax, some with the alignment of text on the page. Tom and I agreed that we wanted to preserve the defining characteristics of Shuri's poetry (and of the Japanese language in general), even when doing so risked a certain oddness in the English translation. When the subject of a verb in Japanese was elided, we honored that construction, left out the subject in English, and began our sentence with the verb. When the poem in Japanese included a greater degree of ambiguity and abstraction than is common in English, we didn't simplify it. We agreed that we would avoid the kind of translation that tries to forcibly stuff the glorious difference of another language's features into the polished shoe of conventional English. In the last stages of our translation, as we prepared the text for Copper Canyon, the editor Elaina Ellis made a number of critical suggestions, and so did copyeditor Rowan Sharp. And then, the astonishing proofreader David Caligiuri trained his three eyes on the manuscript and showed us what we had missed.

Names and Rivers is the first book in English by Shuri Kido. It is likely not a very familiar poetry to its American audience, but we consider that a good thing. The artist Ed Ruscha said that when we encounter not-so-great art, we say, "Wow! Huh?" But when we encounter the real thing, the significant art or writing that we aren't prepared for, we say, "Huh? Wow!" We hope that what sustains your reading of this book is the reaction of that second kind.

Forrest Gander

Shuri Kido was born in 1962 in Morioka, Japan, through which the Kogawa River, a distributary of the Kitakami River, flows. Although time, like rivers, is thought to flow in one direction, in literature it is often a swirling eddy in which poets (and others) from East and West—the long dead and the contemporary—meet.

Profoundly shaped by the exchange of influence between Japanese and American poets through the centuries, Kido's writing is situated in what he calls the "flow of time." The history of mutual influence between Japanese and American poets is fascinating and, in many ways, circular. Many American poets associated with the Beat Generation—including Kenneth Rexroth, Robert Creeley, and Allen Ginsberg—famously visited Japan and influenced a generation of Japanese poets such as Kazuko Shiraishi and Gozo Yoshimasu. In turn many Beat poets, including Philip Whalen, Jack Kerouac, Joanne Kyger, and Gary Snyder, were deeply influenced by Japanese poetry. Preceding the Beat movement, a midcentury friendship between Ezra Pound and Kitasono Katue had a crucial impact on the modernist poetic landscape in both countries.

Shuri Kido, "the far north poet," emerged from these crossed streams. Once when I was talking on the phone with Kido, I casually asked him how he was influenced by Ezra Pound. His answer was, "How can you be influenced by such an enormous poet!? Pound is too big to be influenced by!" Just the same, Kido's poetry is undeniably in conversation with Pound and his concept of "synchronic time."

In *The Spirit of Romance,* Ezra Pound wrote:

> All ages are contemporaneous. . . . The future stirs already in the minds of the few. This is especially true of literature, where the real time is independent of the apparent, and where many dead men are our grand-children's contemporaries, while many of our contemporaries have been

already gathered into Abraham's bosom, or some
more fitting receptacle.

Shuri Kido too explores time "independent of the apparent." For example, in Kido's poem "Ritual Utensils," we encounter Serunbato, a man who traveled from his home in Mongolia to Morioka, just before World War II. Stranded due to the fighting, Serunbato became exiled from his native country. Mr. Serunbato's experiences in Mongolia began to mix with his new experiences in Japan so that there came to be two places inside him, two epochs, a dialogic time.

> "Look—that man!
> That's Mr. Serunbato. The one
> who arrived from the desert just before the war broke out,
> so now he can't go home.
> He wasn't much acquainted with 'water,'
> but now he bathes every day,
> he washes his body
> and watches the river go by."

Having emigrated from the Mongolian desert to a country where water is abundant, Mr. Serunbato came to love the Japanese ritual of taking a bath every day, even more than many locals. One life flowed over another, each miscible, in a constant present tense.

In the middle of the twentieth century, a New Jersey doctor wrote an epic poem employing time/river flow as a metaphor. That doctor-poet, William Carlos Williams, described in *Paterson* the river as "reminiscent of episodes—all that any one man may achieve in a lifetime." This metaphoric association led to what came to be called the "geographical imagination." Soon after Williams's *Paterson,* Jack Kerouac and Gary Snyder also explored time as geography. Kerouac's *On the Road* enacted the passage of time by letting his characters speak while driving or walking; so space—the distance traveled—comes to mark time. Snyder's *Turtle Island* recognized the passage of geologic time in the strata of mountains he saw right in front of him.

Shuri Kido, probing a similar geographical imagination, was also deeply touched by Williams's time/river poetics. This is apparent in poems such as "Kozukata (The Road Never to Be Taken)."

Sadato Bridge crossing over the Kogawa River.
As your body pushes painfully forward, step by step,
it seems you might not reach the other side,
but what you are aiming for is autumn.

Using the geography of his birthplace, Morioka, Kido introduces "you" as the vehicle that crosses the time/river construct. But it may be that "you" will never reach the other side. So what kind of *time order* does Kido imagine?

In "Nonferrous," Kido further enacts a geographical imagination, illustrating time as an encompassing palimpsest. It begins:

NOT NONFERROUS,
all colors mixed to render
the color "gray."

The first line is a vigorous proclamation of Kido's intent to accept everything. Doubling the negatives "not" and "non" to create a positive, Kido accepts even the indistinct "gray" of complex or smudged feelings, observations, intuitions.

The river bites into the land and
"geological memories" surface.
Plants with a grayish tint,
Tillandsia, or remnant snow.
Nothing swaying,
                    nothing wavering,
not a thing too complex to grasp.

Grayish prosaic phenomena,
afloat at the horizon, a cipher, a viper
raises its head.

The world is full of mysteries, but Kido writes that it is, neverthe-
less, "not a thing too complex to grasp." To understand this line, we
might go back to Pound, and his translation of Confucius's *Analects:*

> Said the Philosopher: You think that I have
> learned a great deal, and kept the whole of it in
> my memory?
> Sse replied with respect: Of course. Isn't that
> so?
> It is not so. I have reduced it all to one prin-
> ciple.
> (*Guide to Kulchur,* 15)

In that modernist urge to find a totalizing alembic for meaning,
Pound elucidates that "one principle." He writes:

> We know that history as it was written the day
> before yesterday is unwittingly partial; full of fa-
> tal lacunae; and that it tells next to nothing of
> causes.
> (*Guide to Kulchur,* 31)

It takes time for the lineaments of a historical period to clarify,
for the river to expose "geological memories," as Kido says. According
to Pound, any hasty attempt to historicize "tells next to nothing of
causes." But once "cause" is understood, its counterpart, "effect," can
be intuited. That's how Confucius, Pound, and Kido come to under-
stand the world as "not a thing too complex to grasp."

Kido's "Nonferrous" continues with his own philosophical ques-
tion and answer:

In what country's language does the word "subject"
hold two opposite meanings: "subject OF an action,"
and "subject TO an action"?
There's no such limbo in human memories.

In English, the word *subject* has two opposite meanings, "one
who does something" and "one to whom something is done." Kido
draws our attention to this double meaning to make a philosophical
and poetic point. If words and ideas were the same, there couldn't be
words, such as *stool* or *subject,* that represent more than one meaning.
Aristotle's claim that if there is no single meaning, there is no mean-
ing at all, is problematic. Often, meaning is smudged; it is gray; it
depends upon context and interpretation.

Still, "particles of iron" course through the blood
and all the color drawn from everything
mixes into a "gray"
                    that out of nowhere
stirs up emotions.

It is very difficult to divide Shuri Kido's works in terms of stages.
While each book has its themes, the themes segue into each other.
For example, in 1985's *Shokan* (Shokan—Cited—Cité) and 1993's
Hitetsu (Nonferrous), Kido casts off the overly emotional lyricism
typical of many Japanese poems and creates a new kind of solid lyri-
cism. The books *Kozukata-Sho* (Some Thoughts on Kozukata, 1994),
Moboroshi-no-Haha (The Illusory Mother, 2010), and *Sekai—Kai* (The
World—The Sea, 2010) build on that harder-edged (even scientifically
informed) lyricism and are all concerned with the philosophical rela-
tion between time and the flow of water. Because, at some level, all of
Kido's work takes place in concurrent time, we might say his style of
writing is synchronic in its conception.

Kido is intent upon a new kind of poetry that celebrates the
"gray." It is often out of ambiguity—out of the gray resulting from

a mix of vivid colors, out of the all-at-onceness of perception and intellection—that our emotions rise into consciousness. So it is that between countries and languages, between agonistic and mutualist inclinations, among peers and ancestors, Kido and Pound compose a provocative company. These poems are part of a living conversation in the "flow of time," in the folds between the twentieth and twenty-first centuries.

Tomoyuki Endo

NAMES AND RIVERS

立石寺への

（立石寺への。
ひとまず咽喉から発する脈絡は断て。
結界を越え　揺らぐ、
声の巌 への回峰
すべからく自らの出自を巡り
遂げて（遂げず）　骨林の
鉦にわななき蛇行する
紅彩も浅い呼吸のまま。）

from Shokan—Cited—Cité (1985)

TOWARD TEMPLE RISSHAKU

(Toward Temple Risshaku . . .
For now, swallow back down what your throat coughs up.
The ascetic pilgrimage, crossing the boundary to the sacred place
and wavering there—
your life has been lived among the stony mountains
of voices,
getting your tasks done ((or failing to)),
trembling as the gong resounds through a forest of bones,
meandering.
As scarlet flowers shallowly breathe.)

渇水期

文字に縋る
焚書に星位は狂い
重い掌　指　のあわいから
地誌は洩れ、病む骨相
　（夏の草の間を疾るひとかげを一瞬、）
死せる祖父たちへの禱を身になだれさせ
不眠の　　（有為の）
核へと弓を引く
　（何の宵祭、）
ねじれた垂直面を降りてくるかのごとき母の声
を月光のようなものとして観じ　　（心の）禁圧の
沼に尽くす
仮設の素木　腐蝕のあとを留める銅板にも響く
竹の葉擦れを裂いて
障子をよぎる（見知ったと錯覚した）
女の笑い
　（先行する一行によって）何かが購われているのだろうか
そこに文字のようなものが怯えて見える
つぶらかな甘い歯をした　　（顔のない）
不老の母系が揺すぶっている（のだった）
揺すぶられて
つねに問いへと置換され（また客中………）
冥合はなく谺に搏たれる
　（生まれ………生まれ………）
瓢れ月、蝕の
扉絵を伏せてあらゆる器も朽ちよ
　（化身は斃れ、）
稀には優曇華も見える

4

from Shokan—Cited—Cité (1985)

THE DRY SEASON

All of it dependent on words.
    When books burn,
    even the settings of stars collapse,
    and slipping from thick palms and fingers,
    the history of *place* falls away,
    even the structure of the human body goes wrong.
    (At this moment a figure passes quickly over the summer grass.)
    Letting the blessings of ancestors fall on the body,
    drawing a bow toward the sleepless (karmic) core.
    (What is this festival eve for?)
    Recognizing, as something like moonlight,
    the maternal voice of origin as it ricochets through time's
        connotations
    and sinks (into the mind).
A word, unseasoned wood.
A woman's laughter floats out
    from bamboo leaves that rustle
        in a kind of rhyme with the strumming of grooves
                                in a copper board
    as she passes behind the sliding door
    of half-transparent Japanese paper
    (although I recognize her for what she is).
    Is anything redeemed (by one preceding line)?
    Something like words can be imagined, trembling,
    the long genealogy of our mother tongue,
    each phoneme standing clear (without its face)
    (having been) arousing, aroused,
        to be aroused always, back to certain questions (echoing back)
    never finished, but nested in echoes.

千年の葬礼に盈ち　　（放たれ）
馴らすことはできない
　（炎のようなものだった………）
だが庇護もことばからだとは
　（与えられるとは）　　もう、
わたしが呼んでいる、のではない

(Being born . . . being born . . .)
O moon, come back from your eclipse! Melt down
the utensils in my hands,
mute the images passing against the sliding door!
(The incarnation diminishing.)
Only occasionally can the *udumbara* flowers be seen.
Stuffed with thousands of years of funeral services, (released)
yet still untamed
(a flicker of something like flames . . .).
But an assurance, in words or body,
(never to be given)
is something I cannot even ask for.

祭文

　もう何も書く必要はないはずだ　私の（他者の）名で
さえも　何も書く必要はないはずだ　もう、と呟きな
がら生垣の封印を巡れば人のあるところ蕁麻《いらくさ》は繁茂
する　あり得ない姿態を望むな、と歯擦りを発する
像《かたち》の猫におまえは猫だとの言辞を施しイタドリの葉を
噛んで眺望の罅をいとおしむ（者も私の影だろうか）
　　つねにある余白で　何かの映画を観たばかりの子供
たちが「公園」と名指される場所で猫を縛り首にして
いる　やがて撓んでいた枝は撥ね上がり絶命する（だ
が、何が………）　　何が何を呼んだというのだろうか
　　根の飢餓に隔たる　封印木《シジラリア》をうって　紙には書けな
いものが金平糖の突起をもつ形状で損なっている　ア
スファルトに引かれてゆっくりと沈む脚　（ひとつの
顔）鼓膜を覆い口蓋に甘く熱い記憶を蘇らせて　シ
テ、シテ、濡れてつややかな唇をまるくして涯てる肉
体に力ない言葉を送り翳のたまりを波打たす　ゆるや
かな棺衣を曳いて流れ着く　緑の海に放たれる　綴ら
れることのない幻の自叙伝　まず「私は」と、次には
「離《さか》ってしまった」と白紙の上の書き文字は読めるだ
ろう　そしてその筆跡は誰も示しはしないのだった
　（辞林に迷い、）呼びあってにぶいまどろみをうばわれ
て声はくるしむ　明るすぎる海　投石をさらう海流へと
　　何かの「モリ」と云う不可解（不明）な文字を残して
　（私の）他者は葉むらに失踪する　　ここで打たれる無益
な句読点、　（熱の記憶………）

PRAYER FOR RITUALS

No need to write anymore.   Even my (or another's) name. Murmuring "No more . . . ," turning at the end of the hedge, finding that nettles infiltrate every place people live. Don't expect some impossible perspective, you're merely a cat, speaking to the figure of another cat grinding its teeth. Biting knotweed, mooning over the image of the world in the curve of a cup on which falls (is this my own?) shadow.   At that margin (everywhere it exists) called "a park," some kids, soon after watching a movie, decide to hang a cat. Soon, the bough bounces, and the cat's life flickers out (but what is it that loses its life?). What calls for what?   Stamp the *Sigillaria,* that sealing wood, onto whatever you want to keep. What can't be written on paper must be passed over—along with the trifles of every day. A footprint inscribed in hot asphalt.   With their ears stopped, someone('s face) relives sweet, hot memories that cling to the roof of the mouth.   Cité, Cité (cited, cited), rounding the lips, dispatching powerless words toward the declining body, beckoning to pools of shade.   Drawing the loose shroud and so: drifted away,   released to the green ocean,   the autobiography never having been or going to be written,   the hand-scrawled words on white paper should be read first as *I* and then as *have been away.*   And finally a trace of the brush's stroke delineates nobody.   (Lost in the forest of words)   voices that go nowhere, one calling to another, stopless, suffering. The oceans— too bright.   Oceans toward which the current drags your thrown stone.   Leaving behind the incomprehensible (unknown), the word "mori," (my) otherness lost behind a bush.   And then a useless period is positioned there (behind memories of heat . . .)

逍遙遊篇

　　　　　　　　吉岡実追悼

＜ミューミュー＞と　　鹿は鳴く
　　　　　　　　　　　　　　絵画の
松葉を添えて　客人(まろうど)として降り立っては
天変のための眼で
　　　　　　　　　　地異を受肉しているのだ
朝(あした)の光のもとで　玉石を積み。
その頭上を浮遊する渦鞭毛虫類
ペリジニウス、あるいは
　　　　　　　　　　　　（精霊？）
　　　　　　　　林は透けつつ。
朱絹(あけぎぬ)を骨は纏(まと)う
顎(おとがい)のあたりに抹消のキイを持ち、人外に
後背へ、と出て行く眼差、
　　　　　　　　　　　詩人？
夜明けには茄子を摘みに行く
午後には揺れる、瓢簞の下で眠り
ふたつの実をキリキリと磨いて　夜になれば
言葉が「映るようにする」
　　　　　　　　　　　　　生涯の夏至
世界を覆うのは沈黙である
世紀末の花粉症を抱えて　青麦の波打つ
女体を想像せよ　　　　（骨の）
残影はただよい。

from Nonferrous (1993)

WANDERING BEYOND

a eulogy for Minoru Yoshioka

The deer croon, "Miew, miew"—
                    Who arrives
as a stranger with a pine bough
from a picture,
with one eye foreseeing cataclysms falling from the sky,
cataclysms that hatch open here on Earth?
Under the morning sun, piling up round pebbles.
Above his head flows a stream of peridinian
plankton, "dinoflagellates," or
         (a form of spirit)?
              The woods go transparent. Some
scarlet silk pulled over a skeleton.
His lips a Delete key, his eye pulling
back from and focused behind the company of others—
                    some poet?
At dawn, going out to pick eggplants,
and in the afternoon, napping under
the swaying double-peaked gourds, and later polishing one until it shines,
and then at night, finding words "reflected" on its surface.
                    The summer solstice of a life.
What prevails of the world is its silence.
Suffering hay fever at the end of the century,
imagining a female body where green barley waves.
While the afterimage (of a skeleton?) floats by.

失題

    I

冷え冷えとする
　　　　　　幻の伽藍
神経情報を停止する（毒）のような
一冊の本のなかに閉じ込もり
ヒエロニムス・ボッシュが描く
＜不完全な荒野＞の夏を
透かして見る
　　　　　　暁_{あかつき}
高茎草は伸び
　　　　　　　抽象的作業　たとえば
漢字（ミーニング・レター）の配列は
狂い始める
そこからこそ始まる
　　　　　　　　"母子分離"
遅い河で甜瓜_{まくわうり}を拾い
掌_{てのひら}の塩を舐めては
　　　　　　　猪_{やまくじら}を追う
そのとき問われるべき＜海の欠損＞

    II

題すなら「失題」。
三日ほどの思惟の散策や
　　三分ほどの沈黙のうちには
決して獲得できぬ凍土―
だが、そこは地上から最も遠く

THE TITLE LOST

I

The illusory, freezing-cold temple,
retreating into a book, virtually a "poison," as if giving up
on the network of neuronal information,
         at dawn,
glimpsed through the summer of
                  "the imperfect wasteland"
drawn by Hieronymus Bosch,
high stalks of grass going higher and higher;
such abstract labors,
like the arrangement of Chinese characters (ideograms),
become imprecise.
Which is where
            "separation of mother and child" begins.
Picking gourds beside time's slow-flowing river,
licking salt from the palms,
            and chasing wild boars, "mountain whales,"
but then, the "absence of a sea" must be taken into consideration.

II

The title must be "The Title Lost."
The soil so frozen it registers
neither three minutes of silence
            nor three days of contemplative walks, frozen soil—
Or is it a soil so remote
it wouldn't be visible from anywhere on Earth?
Good day, good direction,

そこは地上からはよく見えない
よき日　よき方位
媒介もなしに死者は現れる
忘れていた夏の草の記憶、
　　　　　　　　　　虎杖<ruby>虎杖<rt>いたどり</rt></ruby>？
野原のどこにでもあり
陽炎で輪郭をあいまいにしていた、
まるで人間のように。
ある種の生物は
「過去」の検証に苛まれる

　　　　　III

息絶えるまでつづく踊り、
　　　　　　　<ruby>大舞踏<rt>コレア・マジョール</rt></ruby>
人間はときに奇妙な病いを発明する
非金属には避け難い
　　　　　　可視域の出来事
目に見えるものを好み
目に見えるものに怖れおののく
たとえば、大津波
　　いっさいの前兆もなく。塔のごとき水の壁
　　は押し寄せ、海辺の街を潰滅させる
たとえば、大雪崩
　　海抜八千メートルの山巓は数万トンの雪塊
　　を滑り落とした。白い褥に眠る人、街—
たとえば、大地震
　　小国は揺れて滅びる。地上を地底へと、吸
　　引する意思、マグニチュード八・五。
いかなる招聘？
<ruby>向日性<rt>ヘリオトロープ</rt></ruby>植物は咲く

without intermediaries, and then the dead show up.
Memories of summer grass, freshly recalled,
                              knotweed?
Found everywhere through the field,
its outline blurry with haze,
which is the same case with humans.
Some species are tortured
by their inspections of "the past."

III

Chorea they called St. Vitus's dance, whose afflicted couldn't stop
                              dancing until their last breath.
Humans can, by mistake, invent their own strange diseases.
An accident unavoidable for a nonmetallic species
                              in the realm of the visible.
Attracted to the visible world
and terrified of the visible world.
As such, an enormous tsunami,
        no omen. A wall of water big as a tower
        rushing in, devastating entire towns.
As such, a massive avalanche,
        the top of a mountain 8,000 meters above sea level
        dips its shoulder and releases
        thousands of tons of snow. People, villages
        sleeping under the white cover—
As such, an intense earthquake,
        rattling and devastating a small country. Essentially
        sucking the surface into the bowels of the earth,
        a magnitude of 8.5.
What invitation?
Heliotropic plants bloom.

IV

疾走する身体のようなもの
　　　　　　　　夕陽に歪む（車体）
　古の法典は云う
　　　　　　＜山河定めよ＞
俗曲の調べは響かぬ
　　　　　　　＜肯定的歴史観＞
今、越えるのが
　　　　　　　　—大地溝帯
単調な景色はゆらゆらし
訪れる紛れもない
　　　　　　　＜失郷症＞
失われるのは地名、
それが詩篇。

V

暁は、
　　　意思なき土地をも染め上げる
ルクレツィア、
その肖像の妖しい微笑のような
　　　　　　　　　　　＜雲＞
毎日、数個の無花果をかじっては
飢えをしのぎ
　　　　　生霊
のような（その）雲をアトリエから描く画家
野猫ともいい玉面とも呼びなす
生臭い息の小さな生き物は
暑さでぐったりとする
「白骨」を「自分」と
誤読してしまう日。
いずれにしろ

16

IV

Something such as a human body dashing by,
            or (a car body) distorted by evening's sun.
The ancient laws say:
            "Set borders over mountains and rivers."
That "positivist historical view" which is
                        never celebrated in our folk songs.
Now, crossing over
            —Fossa Magna,
the monotonous scenery shimmering.
Coming along, but
            "*Atopos* = 'without a place' = atopy"
When the name of the place is lost.
That's what "poem" is.

V

Dawn,
            investing the land with color, without intention.
Lucrezia
"the clouds"
like her portrait's mysterious smile;
each day, staving off hunger
chewing a handful of figs,
                        the painter
painting (the) clouds, almost a living spirit,
from the atelier.
A wildcat, or an "alabaster face"
exhaling its stinky breath,
just a small creature
exhausted from the heat.
One day I misread 「白骨 (white bones)」 as 「自分 (myself)」.

nubes（＝雲）は死者の技
どこにも留まらず何者とも交わらぬ。
公孫樹は緑色に炸裂し
傾く夏は
　　　　死者の肩に落ちる。

In some way,
a nimbus practices the art of the dead;
never remaining in one place, it keeps to itself.
Ginkgo trees blare their greenness.
And summer slants
　　　down upon the shoulders of the dead.

北の方位

＜祟り＞なす“荒魂”
わずかな生物しかいない
　　　　　　荒蕪地にも
　　　　　　陽光は落ち
露わにされていく物体、
すなわち、自己の“規格”
だがそれを、他者に委ねる者もいる
「さまよえるオランダ人」のごとき
幽霊に似た＜実体＞。
存在も非在も
　　　　　　“実証の場”では近似したもの
神学的な＜不毛＞がひらける
　　　　　　　　言葉の野—
桃の実はくずれ
　　　　　　　山脈はくずれ
肥沃の地は再生する
それは「空」を描く画稿のように
空間に属しながらも
　　　　　　　　“時間”の範疇
＜あの世＞の部分である
たなびく雲、
積み上がる雲は“奇魂”にも見え
伝言という伝言は信じられない
そのようにして
　　　　　　　一九九〇年は過ぎる
ある種の「場所」
　　　　　　　　もしくは「名」
それらを包含する力場の消失、

20

THE DIRECTION NORTH

"*Ara-Mitama* (the Wild Spirit)" who puts curses on people.
   The sun burns
    over this wasteland
and its few creatures,
the outline of some object coming clearer and clearer,
which you recognize as: "the default" of yourself.
Though there are those who yield it to others.
An "existence" akin to a phantom's, like "the Flying Dutchman,"
for existence and nonexistence
    can both supply substantiation.
A theological "wasteland" yawns
open in the field of language.
Peaches rot,
      mountains crumble,
reviving the fertile soil,
and like drafts on a canvas of "the nothing that is,"
they belong to "space,"
      but also to "time."
A part of "the other world,"
those trailing clouds
and the nimbus piled high to resemble "*Kushi-Mitama* (the Spirit
  of Wisdom),"
message after unreliable message.
In such a way,
    the year 1990 passes.
Some kind of "place,"
    or "name,"
and the disappearance of that field where both interact, then,
      "the void"?

<　失語症　>？

誤謬に満ちた確信に基づいても
たやすく＜精神＞の放浪は遂げられる
存在も非在も
"実証の場"では同義、
悪しき正気であれ　悪しき狂気であれ
正しき正気であれ　正しき狂気であれ
語りつづける者に災いあれ
沈黙が測れぬ者に
　　　　　　　　災いあれ
それが死者の言葉。
訛語なき語彙の
　　　　　　　塔に似た（建造物）に
登っては"碑文"を読み、
雁行する鳥のゆくえを尋ねる
あちらが北、
　　　　　　あちらは北
災いの方位、と。

Although propelled by conviction
rife with fallacy,
the "mind" wanders.
Existence and nonexistence
can both supply substantiation.
May sanity go sane, let sanity go insane.
May insanity go sane, let insanity go insane.
May curses fall on those who keep running their mouths.
May curses fall on those who can't
                              fathom silence.
Such are the words the dead speak.
Scaling the (construction) as though it were a tower
                        of vocabulary without dialects,
reading "*scriptum* (= inscriptions on a stone),"
asking where those skeins of geese are flying.
North is the way,
                  the way
due north,
that cursed direction.

非鉄

非鉄にあらず、
あらゆる色彩を混ぜ合わせると
現れてくる色彩は＜灰＞。
水の方位の涯に
“地質学的記憶”は露出する
灰を帯びた植物、
空中植物もしくは残雪
そよぐものはなく
　　　　　　　　ゆらぐものもなく
この地上に難解なものは存在しない。
灰色の散文的事象
その地平に鎌首をもたげる
蛇のごとき謎。
ある国の言葉では、「主体」という語に
「隷属」もしくは「服従」の意味も孕まれる
人間の記憶にない場所。
そこでも血流に小さな＜鉄の玉＞は混じり、
ゆえ知らぬ感情を
　　　　　　　　波立たせる
あらゆる方位の＜灰＞。

NONFERROUS

NOT NONFERROUS,
all colors mixed to render
the color "gray."
The river bites into the land and
"geological memories" surface.
Plants with a grayish tint,
Tillandsia, or remnant snow.
Nothing swaying,
                    nothing wavering,
not a thing too complex to grasp.
Grayish prosaic phenomena,
afloat at the horizon, a cipher, a viper
raises its head.
In what country's language does the word "subject"
hold two opposite meanings: "subject OF an action,"
and "subject TO an action"?
There's no such limbo in human memories.
Still, "particles of iron" course through the blood
and all the color drawn from everything
mixes into a "gray"
                    that out of nowhere
stirs up emotions.

祭器

あなたは水を汲む。
昨日に似た今日　今日に似た明日
川の源にはすずやかな山があり
淀みには魚も棲み。
掌で水を切るようにして
あなたは水を汲む
時折、冷ややかな流れにその手を切られるようにして。

北の水は薄い。
だから、あなたが抱える壺は
陽の下で影を失っていく
見る夢はすべて悪夢。
この静かな街に九十五の川は流れ
物言わぬ人々が行き交う三百九の橋の下を
川は流れ。
あなたは知っている
浅瀬の秘め事と淀みの謀みを。
時に唇に薄い笑いが掃かれるのは
あなたが人の世から遠ざかっていく印。

あなたには見える。
ひとつの流れとはいえ、幾筋もの水が寄り集うもの。
ある流れは汚穢を運び
ある流れは何も運ばぬ
濡れた足首で、川面を渡る冷えた風に熱を奪われて
どんな意思もない清らかな水を
あなたは汲みつづける
あなたの壺は祭器のように透け、

RITUAL UTENSILS

You draw water.
Yesterday as you did today, today as you will tomorrow.
The headwaters emerge from a range of calm mountains,
fish course through tranquil pools.
As though deflecting the flow with your palm,
you draw water
as though your palm is deflected by the flow.
In the north, water runs thin.
So the vase you hold loses its shadow in sunlight.
Every dream is a nightmare.
Through this small town, ninety-five streams surge,
and 309 bridges cross those streams.
People come and go over them silently.
You're someone who knows
the secrets of the shallows and the conspiracies of the pools.
Sometimes, a bland smile comes to your lips
which can be read as the sign that you've broken free from your ordinary life.

You can see it.
And though it appears as one stream, many smaller streams compose it.
One stream carries mud,
another carries nothing.
Even while your body heat is lifted away from your wet ankles by cold wind
blowing above the river,
you continue to draw clear water
that flows with no other ambition.
Your vase goes transparent as a ritual utensil,
and your body shows no sheen of sweat.
Suddenly the smile drains from your bland, pale face because

あなたの躰には汗も浮かぬ
不意にその生ま白い貌から笑みが消えるのは
水の無感覚に触れる指先が
この世の外に連れ去られそうになるから

あなたが厭うもの
樹、鳥の柔毛、すべて体温のあるもの
そして、言葉。
あなたの愛するもの
摘まれた花、切花、移ろいやすいもの、薄っぺらいもの
とりわけ、濃い影を落とさぬもの。
あなたが飾るのは切花ばかり
日々、水を汲み換えては
衰えていく花とともに月の出を待つ
あなたは多くを語らない
ただ一度、古い橋を過ぎる異人を見た、あのときを除い
　　ては。

この家には手紙も来ない
一本の煙草を吸うほどの緩慢な自死
あなたの壺は祭器に似て
次第に高台が高くなってきたようだ
子が産まれ、子が育ち
種子は芽吹き、森になり
そして、廃れ。
北斗の星も傾く
なのに、なぜ？
あなたは水を汲み
花を生け、自らの身に注ぐ
花は、水によって数日を生き延びる
と人は噂し
あなたは、水が花を殺すと言う

when your fingers make contact with the indifferent water,
you're nearly carried away to the world beyond.
What you despise:
trees, goose down, anything that radiates heat,
and language.
What you love:
picked flowers, cut flowers, whatever fades, slenderness
especially, forms that cast no thick shadows.
Only cut flowers, which you arrange.
Every day, you change the vase's water
and wait for the moon to rise.
You talk very little,
except on that occasion when you came across the foreigner
crossing the old bridge.

No letters reach your house.
The slow suicide of another cigarette.
The well of your vase, so high above its base,
resembles a Korean ritual vessel.
Children are born, children grow,
seeds take root, budding out into forests,
and then die.
The seven stars up in the northern sky tilt.
But still, I'm curious why
you draw water,
arrange flowers, douse yourself.
Water allows cut flowers to live a few more days,
they say,
but you argue that water drowns flowers.
Your flowers, I remember, were diaphanous as an antlion's wings:
even in sunlight they cast no shadow.

On the northern waters whose murmurs can't be heard,
yesterday's shadows fall, today's shadows flow off;

そういえば　あなたの花は薄羽のようで
陽が差しても影も落ちぬ

せせらぎも聴こえぬ北の水に
昨日の影が落ち、今日の影は流れ
あなたは唇に薄い笑いを掃く
上手には夕顔瀬橋、
夜な夜な影のない女が立つと云う

「見て、あの人を。
あれがセルンバトさん。
砂漠からやって来て、戦争が起って
もう帰れなくなったんだわ
彼は水が珍しいの
だから毎日お風呂に入って
からだをすすいでいるんだわ
そして、ああやって
ずっと川を見ているんだわ」
それは誰に聞かせるためでもない
あなたのいちばん長いモノローグ
薄い水は人影をようやく川面に映すばかり。

あなたは水に囚われぬ
あなたは水を汲み
自らの身に注ぐ
昨日に似た今日は去り、
今日に似た明日をめぐり。
そのために、あなたは水を汲む
静けさを削り取るように九十五の川は流れ
川の淀みには息をせぬものたちが棲み
川の浅瀬には息を荒らすあなたが立ち
あなたの躰は薄羽のようで
陽が差しても影も落ちぬ。

you wipe the bland smile from your lips.
Up there is Yugaose Bridge,
upon which, night after night, they say, a woman stands apart from
      her shadow.

"Look—that man!
That's Mr. Serunbato. The one
who arrived from the desert just before the war broke out,
so now he can't go home.
He wasn't much acquainted with 'water,'
but now he bathes every day,
he washes his body
and watches the river go by."
That's your longest monologue, and meant for no one.
The transparent water barely holds anyone's shadow to its surface.

Elusive water.
You draw it up,
pour it over yourself.
Today courses by like yesterday,
today floats like a cork on tomorrow.
And that's why you draw water.
As though scoring the silence, ninety-five streams flow,
and in the pool something breathless lives,
panting, there in the shallows of the river, where you stand,
your body like the thin wings of an antlion,
casting no shadow under the sun.
Your vase, going more transparent still,
is filled with dead, mute water.
Your flowers, day by day, transparentize,
water rots them; it was you who said so.
You draw water,
your body rinsed of human scent,
the bodies of creatures in the pool growing colder,

いよいよ透けていくあなたの壺には
音も立てぬ死んだ水が満ち。
あなたの花は、日々、衰えていく
水が腐らせるもの、そう言ったのはあなた。
人の匂いもしない躰で
あなたは水を汲む
淀みに棲むもののからだも冷え
枯死することなく花は衰え
あなたは衰え。

壺も衰え。

the flowers going transparent, not wilting;
you go transparent.

The vase, too, goes transparent.

解題

　北国の人々の水に対する感受性、それは南方とは随分と異ったものである。北の水の清冽さは、決して人の肌になじもうとするものではない。たとえ、水道の水であっても一年を通じて手を凍らすほどの冷気を湛えている。それゆえに川縁を散策する人の姿も、わずかに釣糸を垂れる人を除いては、あまり見かけることがない。

　セルンバト氏は実在の人物で、すでに故人。十五年戦争のさなかに岩手農専（現岩手大学農学部）に留学し、戦争の勃発のため帰国の途を断たれて、そのまま盛岡で暮らしていたという。砂漠から来た彼にとって、水で身体を洗うという贅沢は、よほど気に入った習俗らしく、若い日には、毎日のように洗面器を抱えて銭湯に通う彼の姿を見かけたものだと伝え聞く。結局、彼は盛岡の女性を娶り、川に恵まれた盆地の街で、その生涯を終えた。

　数奇な人生を送った砂漠の人と、その生前、私は話を交したことがない。

The sensitivity regarding water, cultivated by those in northern countries, is generally different from that of those living in southern countries. The crystal-clear quality of water in the north never quite stops feeling shocking to human skin. Even tap water stays cool throughout the year, chilling the hands. So you don't see many people, aside from a few fishermen, along the river.

Mr. Serunbato came to Morioka to study at Iwate Agricultural School (now Iwate University, Faculty of Agriculture) during the Asia-Pacific War, and he had no way to go back home. A denizen of the desert, he came to love the luxury of bathing. People saw him almost every day walking to the public bath holding his basin, they say. He never returned to his native land, but married a woman and lived out his life in Morioka, where water is so abundant.

That desert man who led such an unusual life, he and I never had a chance to talk.

不来方
<small>こずかた</small>

涸川を渡るのは貞任橋、
<small>さだとう</small>
いつまでも対岸に届かぬ軀を
つらそうに　少しずつ
追いやるようにして
あなたが追うのは、秋。
山郭は依々として
鳥もけものも午睡のうちにある
粧いも淡く紅だけあかく
<small>よそお</small>
戯れに真似てみるには
あまりに鮮やかな偽絵のよう

川の名は諸葛川、
<small>もろくず</small>
あなたは指折り数えるが
何もかもうろおぼえで。
もう会うこともないから、と
左右に分かれていく雲に似て
水系は伸び
いくつもの橋を流し去っていく

あなたは指折り数えるが
ほそい指は今しがた
川の魚の腹をなでたようで
清い瀞を思わせる
<small>とろ</small>
あなたは順に指を折る
せいしゅん、青春。
せきか、　　赤夏。
はくしゅう、白秋。
げんとう、　玄冬。

KOZUKATA (THE ROAD NEVER TO BE TAKEN)

Sadato Bridge crossing over the Kogawa River.
As your body pushes painfully forward, step by step,
it seems you might not reach the other side,
but what you are aiming for is autumn.

The shape of the mountains, vague,
birds and animals half-asleep.
Your makeup light but for a splash of crimson red
that, were we to encounter it in a painting, would seem unreal.
Here, it's called the Morokuzu River.
You try counting on your fingers
but nothing adds up, you can't remember.
"I won't meet them anymore," you say,
and just as clouds mass across the sky,
the water masses and
washes out the bridges.

You count, folding your skinny fingers
to your palm until it seems you're touching
the belly of a fish in the river,
which calls to mind the image of a clear pool.
Folding your fingers one by one:
the pale spring,
the ruby summer,
the white autumn,
the dark winter.
Are they seasons
or the episodes of a life?
And you, with your pinky still unfolded, say,

それは季節、それとも一生？
あなたは最後の小指を立てたまま
「それだけ」と口にする
それだけ、ただ生きているだけ。
駒ヶ岳から水は生じ
雫石川を水は流れ
川面には小さな筏が浮かぶ
あれは、百年前のまぼろし。

あなたの影は
方丈の隅に潜む闇のよう
陸稲に蜻蛉がまどうころ
夏だから生まれる者がいて、
夏だから息絶える者がいて。
あなたが渡るのは三馬橋、
小心な橋を踏み抜かぬように
自失の身を運ぶなら
北上の淵に銀の腹を見せるのは
朱を刷いたうぐい、そして、あゆ
生まれなかった子供。
あなたは橋を行く
誰に命じられたわけでもなく
あなたがそうしているのが
千年の血の裔の証し―

けれども、
渡河する姿は死人のよう
残された小指のよう。
誰もが目を伏せるのは
戯れに真似てみるには
その立ち姿が
あまりにあの世に近すぎるから。

"That's all that's given."
You're alive in this now, in this world.
The Komagatake Mountain births the water
flowing into the Shizukuishi River,
upon whose surface small rafts float,
an illusion from one hundred years before.

Your shadow is like darkness itself
squatting in the corner
of a ten-by-ten hut.
When dragonflies rise above rice fields,
some just hatched,
some dropping away,
it's summer.
Sanma Bridge, you cross it,
hauling your lost body with you,
careful not to step through the timorous planks;
on the surface of the Kitakami River, below,
flash the red-flushed silver bellies of minnows, ayu—sweetfish—
and unborn children.
You pass over the bridge;
following nobody's orders,
you make the crossing.
Testament to a bloodline going back eons.

But still,
your figure crossing over looks like a shade,
like a pinky held up in the air.
Everyone fixes you in their gaze,
your bearing too marked by the other world
to be considered casually.

The view opens only along the river,
and this is such a place.

川筋だけに伸びていく眺望、
ここはそれだけの土地
筏流しが陸揚げされる土手に
残されるのは治水の碑
花崗岩の石積みをすすいで
静かに川は流れる
それも、百年前のまぼろし
よノ字橋、毘沙門橋を過ぎて
あなたは指折り数えるが
確かなものは何もなくて
そのくせあまりに鮮やかで。
いずれ、百年前のまぼろし

それとも―
編まれた地理が伝える
贋の過去？
遮られることに応じて道は折れ
耳の奥には
山鳴りが響きつづけるから
「あれは死人。」
針葉の先にぼおっとともる
あおい光を指さして
あなたは指を折る
せいしゅん、せきか、はくしゅう、げんとう
たたずむなら鑪山橋、
ふと気づくと
人生が終わっていたとでもいうように
無音の世界は広がって
鳥もけものも
醒めることのない午睡のうちにある
川が立てる落魄の音に
亡家の音も消え。
「このあたりの者」と

On the near bank where log-rafters land
they've erected a monument to flood control.
The river goes on its way silently
swishing over granite stonework.
That, too, is an illusion one hundred years old.
Beyond Yonojibashi Bridge, and Bishamon Bridge,
you count on your folding fingers the number of bridges.
Though nothing is certain,
everything is vivid.
In times to come, this also will be an illusion one hundred years old.

Or—
was an artificial past
sewn into this woven topography?
The road twists around impediments,
the rumbling of the mountain reverberates
deep in my ears:
"The sound of the dead calling."
You, pointing out the vague shimmer
playing along the tops of pine needles,
fold your fingers.
The pale spring, the ruby summer, the white autumn, the dark winter.
As you linger on Rozan Bridge,
the mute world stretches out, as though a life has finished,
birds and animals stuck in their wakeless nap.
The sounds made by a rickety family living along the river,
those vibrant sounds have faded away.
They would have said,
"We're the natives of this place,"
because their own country had been lost
long before.
The city's name, Kozukata,
derives from an ancient promise
never to take the road there again.

応答は限られて
あなたがたに
郷里は失われて久しいと云う
その街の名を、不来方。
それは二度と訪れぬという
古の誓いの残した名。
あなたはふと気づくと
自分の生が終わっていたとでもいうように
淡い粧いで橋を行く
戯れに真似てみるには
あまりに鮮やかな偽絵のようで
誰に命じられたのでもなく
あなたはまるで死人のよう
清らな淵や瀞に
破鏡のさざなみは立ち。
今、誰かが身を投げる
それも、百年前のまぼろし。

You pass, unnoticed, over the bridge,
wearing light makeup,
as though your life were over,
your bearing so marked
that if it were rendered on canvas
it wouldn't be convincing,
no one could intend it,
you resemble a shade.
Over the clear river's pools,
ripples quiver, a broken bundle of mirrors.
And now, someone leaps into the water,
though that, too, is an illusion from one hundred years ago.

解題

　盛岡の古名である。その由来は、「覚え書き」に記した。

　その呼び方は、今日、盛岡で暮らす人々にとっても、それほど親しいものではない。わずかに江戸時代に、そのあたり一帯を領した南部氏の居城が、石垣だけを残す史跡公園となっており、不来方城跡と呼ばれることがあるくらいだろうか。かつて、石川啄木は次のような一首を詠んだ。＜不来方のお城の草に寝ころびて空に吸はれし十五の心＞。

　啄木歌集中、とりたてて問題とすべき一首ではない。ただ、頭上の空との対峙のうちに、帰郷譚に囚われた晩年の啄木とは異質の解放があるばかりである。

　故郷を出て行くこと。そして再び故郷に帰っていくこと。近代的な喪失と回帰の物語を、「二度と来ない所」という意味の古名、不来方は拒否している。いわば、その名で呼ばれる土地は、あらかじめ失われてある故郷なのだと言えるだろうか。

AUTHOR'S NOTE TO "KOZUKATA (THE ROAD NEVER TO BE TAKEN)"

Kozukata is the ancient name for the city of Morioka. In my "Note to *Some Thoughts on Kozukata*," I've written about the origins of its name.

The ancient name is not so familiar, even with the residents of Morioka. The stonework of the castle from the Edo period, built by the Nanbu clan who reigned over the region, is now a historical site called Kozukata. Ishikawa Takuboku, the tanka poet, composed a song that goes: "Lying on the grass at the Kozukata Castle site, / drawn into the sky, / my fifteen-year-old heart."

The contrast between the poet's mentality and the sky above him is striking. And the poem has an openness in regard to Takuboku's obsession with the thought of returning to his homeland in his later years.

Leaving the homeland. And coming back to the homeland. The ancient name Kozukata, meaning "the direction never to be visited" or "the road never to be taken," cuts off the modern story of losing and then returning to the homeland. Instead, the homeland is lost from the start.

覚え書き

　私は北の小都邑で生まれた。東と西を山系に挟まれた盛岡は、川に恵まれた山あいの地方であり、高地特有の低い空と北国特有の深々とした針葉の緑に囲まれた静かな街である。中津川と北上川が合流するところに、石垣だけの城跡を残すその街の古名を、不来方と云う。

　不来方は、二度と来ない所という意味であり、その地名のいわれは次のように語られている。時も知れぬ上代に、飛来して大地に突き立った三つの火山弾が、いつしか神体として人々の信仰を集めるようになり、三ツ石の神と呼ばれるようになった。ところが、時代を経て、鬼が現われ、しばしば里人を苦しめたので、人々は三ツ石の神に祈り、悪鬼を捕えてもらった。鬼は恐れおののき、二度とこの土地に来ないことを誓い、その証として三ツ石に手形を残して去ったのだと伝承は伝える。巨石に残された手形から、「岩手」という地名が生じ、二度と来ないと誓った場所であるということから、「不来方」という呼び名が生じた。それが、口伝のあらましである。

　二十代の終わりから、私にとっても故里は、時折、訪れるところでしかなくなった。久方の帰郷のたびに、私は「不来方」という地名のいわれを想い起こす。その山河は、なつかしいもの以上に、痛ましい。それは、ただ、たんに自分のいささかの感傷を反映しているだけなのかも知れぬ、だが、私は、郷里の土を踏むたびに、そこが二度と訪れるべき場所ではなかったことを確認するのだった。

　しかし、実のところ、「郷里」と名指される特権的な土地への違和にとどまりつづけようとすることは、「郷里」への順当な親和を生きることと同じていどにた

46

I was born in a small city in the north, Morioka, which lies between east–west mountain ranges. A quiet city with the kind of low sky typically seen in highlands, it is surrounded by the deep green of coniferous forests that are indigenous to northern countries. The city, known for its drinking water, is located where the Nakatsu River and the Kitakami River merge. Its ancient name is Kozukata, and an ancient castle's stonework is still a part of the city.

As for the story of the name Kozukata, "the direction never to be visited" or "the road never to be taken," legend has it that a long time ago, three spindle bombs from a volcanic eruption formed three stone mounds, known as Mitsuishi-no-Kami, "the gods of Three Stones," that were worshipped by the locals. Later, goblins appeared and tormented the people, who prayed to the gods to capture the goblins. The gods did, and the goblins were so terrified that they promised never to return to the land. As a proof of their promise, they left handprints on the Three Stones before they departed. Hence the name of the prefecture where I was born: Iwate, literally meaning "rock hand."

I was near the end of my twenties when I realized that the so-called homeland is the place where I sometimes "visit." Every time I visit the city, I remember the origin of the ancient name Kozukata. Watching the mountains and rivers, I always feel more wounded than nostalgic. That may be because I feel sentimental, but every time I visit the place, I recognize it as a road never to be taken.

As it turns out, to continue to feel out of place in my so-called homeland is not so different from feeling an easy familiarity with it. Going back to the origin of the word "nostalgia," I learned that it's a coined word linking "*nostos*" (homecoming) and "*algos*" (pain). Inspired by Sakutaro Hagiwara's *Kyodo Bokei Shi* (Poems Looking toward My Homeland), I began writing poems whose geography

やすいものでしかない。ノスタルジー (nostalgia) とは、その語源を辿るならば「帰還」(nostos) の「苦しみ」(algos) にほかならないのだから。適度な距離を措いた遠景として「郷里」をやり過ごさぬために、ある時期から、萩原朔太郎の「郷土望景詩」をならって、時折、盛岡の風水を背景にした詩作を試みるようになった。しかし、詩篇は、朔太郎のそれとは大きく隔って、いささかの望むべき眺望も現われることはなく、かわりに、「あなた」と名指される幻のような女性を生むこととなった。一篇ごとに別人の相貌しか見せぬ「あなた」とは、いったい誰なのか。そして、その女性の幻像が、何を秘めるのかは、私にも判然としない。彼女は、凍った叙情をその身にまとうようにして、忘れたころに私を訪れ、いつの間にか去っていく。ただ、たしかなのは、これらの過激に叙情を仮装する詩篇が、ひたすら、何かを捨て去ろうとしていることだけである。

一九九二年、冬

served as a distant background. Yet my poems are totally different from Hagiwara's. Not even one "desirable view" appeared. Instead, what I encountered was an illusory woman called "you." Who is this "you" whose features vary from poem to poem? And what does the illusory existence of this woman mean if even I, the poet, don't know? This woman, with her frozen lyricism, visited me again when I had almost forgotten her, and then she disappeared. The only thing that is certain is that these poems, under this extremely lyrical disguise, try to shuck off something.

白の肖像

雲に放火した
とでもいうような正午、
昇っていく空は天頂ににあって
今、一気になだれ落ちようとする
地上では
野火のように静かに広がる
流言蜚語が
人心を強アルカリに似た方法で蝕む
むしろ　コバルトの炎と化した
空を見よ。
そこにもし一片の"骨"を置くとしたら
その白さは痛いほど、
目に沁むだろう
卵を抱くように肩を抱き
想像しがたい孤独に震える、
人間という生き物の
稲妻のごとき屈折。
その深度をはかっては
夏草のごとく繁茂していく＜時間＞
頭を抱えて深酒したり
膝を抱いてうずくまったりする
「人間」の煩悶あるいは苦悩と呼ばれる
情動は　隠喩に等しく
影を折りたたみ　闇を肉体に溶かしていく
そのうえで暗闇に染まらぬ
"骨"の白さを讃えよ
空の青さが
散骨という風習の起源だとしたら

THE PORTRAYAL OF WHITE

Noon came and it was
as though the clouds caught fire.
The sky piling into its zenith,
and now, "now" might be dispelled in an instant.
On this earth,
wild rumors quietly take off
like brush fires,
and they scorch us like strong alkali.
It could be you'd prefer to watch the sky
turning into a cobalt conflagration.
And if "a piece of bone" were hung there,
its whiteness would make your eyes ache.
Cupping your own shoulders as you might cup an egg,
you shudder, imagining a loneliness beyond your imagination.
A torn, jagged idea, like a thunderbolt,
sourced in the cloud of our species.
Measuring the depth of the emotion,
"time" fans out like summer grass.
Holding your head, drinking heavily,
holding your knees, curling into a ball;
the human emotions "agony" or "anguish"
are metaphors for "time,"
the shadows folding, the darkness dissolving into body.
Then, praise for "the bone's" whiteness
which never quite fades into the surrounding dark.
If we associate blue with "bone-scattering" rituals,
is the whiteness of bone a metaphor for "time"
or a compelling mimicry of what only adheres to the "surface"?
This noon,

骨の白さは時の比喩、
あるいは優れた"表面"の模倣だろうか
この正午、
七日目の休日により深く
"灰"のように眠る
小さな生き物は
起こりえないことを夢見ては
寝返りを打つ
誰も知らずとも咲く花椰菜（ハナヤサイ）。
雲が鴇色（ときいろ）に染っても
何色にも染まりえぬ
白さの肖像のあちこちに
＜時間＞は滞留し始める。

even more deeply than on the seventh day,
a small creature sleeps like "ashes"
dreaming of something that never happens,
turning its body.
Cauliflowers, or cabbage flowers, bloom, though no one observes them.
When clouds are colored with the same pale rose seen on the wings
                                        of the Japanese ibis,
"time" holds, filling with that "white" light
in which all colors in the visible spectrum are contained.

千の母音

長い坂道だった
強い日差しも傾いて落ちていた
いつまで歩いても"途中"だった
名はちりぢりに裂けていった
ひたすら登っていくだけで
私も名前を忘れ去っていた
西風がタイフーンの進路を変え
世界は数時間の混乱のうちにある。
名づけても名づけても
すぐさまその名を失っていくものを
私たちは「自然」と呼ぶから
私はそのただなかにいた。
何かが欠けている、
そのことの皮膜のように。
母音が千に飛び散って
名が欠けていた
荒涼をきわめるヴィジョンに
再び自然という名を与える
その名は次の瞬間から風化を始める
名を失いつつあるものと
名を失ったものとが
鮮やかな起伏を織り成して
本当の名を告げていた
翼あるものは伏せていた
誰にも聞こえない叫びをあげて
人とはなんと壊れやすいのか、
と何度も名のりながら
千の波紋が

A THOUSAND VOWELS

A long slope.
The strong sun dipped, and finally sank.
No matter how long I walked, I stayed in "the middle of the road."
The name torn to pieces.
Just keeping on, climbing higher and higher,
I'd completely forgotten the name.
The west wind shifts the typhoon's course;
the world, for a few hours, is thrown into confusion.
You might name one thing after another,
but each loses its name in that same moment.
Into what we call "nature."
I stood in the middle of nature.
And something was missing, the natural was
draped in a thin shroud.
Vowels scattered,
the name went missing.
When once more the name "nature" was applied
to the desolate-as-ever landscape,
immediately, the name began to weather away.
What is still losing its name
and what has already lost its name,
those two strands entwine
around the true name.
Those who have wings stay put,
howling out their condition over and over,
"How fragile we are!"
though no one hears them.
Thousands of ripples tell
a story of benthic anguish.

海面下の苦悩を伝えている
海底の決潰を教えている
波紋の行きつくはてに
それぞれの名前があって
地上に　母音が千に飛び散った。

The ripples beach themselves
on the name of each anguish,
vowels scatter by the thousands
over the earth.

不安の慣性^{イナーシア}

本当は私が語ることができるのは
苦痛についてだけなのかも知れない
心が壊れていく音や
その静けさやゆるやかさについて、
それだけなのかも知れない。
月が銀色に濡れていた。
孤独だなどということは、
あまりにたやすいことだった。
孤独でさえなかった。
そのころチャタム諸島の深海には
巨大なイカが遊泳していた。
プランクトンを食べ、小魚を食べ
やがては同類を、大型魚を呑み
次第に次第に肥大していった
深海はあまりに淋しくて
その淋しさの分だけ軀に
アンモニアを貯えながら
透明ではなくなっていった、
ゆるやかに濁っていった。
今ならば、私にも分かるだろう
その名よ、あまりに身近なものよ。
孤独だなどということは
たかが知れていた
絶望と名づけても
ありふれたものだった。
つまらないものと私は戦っていた。
その名を静かにささやくと
ひとりでに孤独と絶望の

58

THE INERTIA OF ANXIETY

The only thing I can talk about may be
the pain,
the sound of the soul shattering into pieces,
and how quietly or how sluggishly it happens—
that may be the only thing.
The moon wet and silvered.
Being lonely
was such an easy thing.
But I wasn't even lonely.
Around this time, a huge squid
was circulating in the Chatham Island deeps.
Feeding on plankton, small fish,
and its own solitude, tearing apart larger fish,
putting on size.
It was so lonely in the deep sea
that the squid became less and less transparent
as ammonia collected in its system,
that and loneliness.
By then, I recognized
the word, a term close to me.
"Being lonely" was imaginable enough,
but calling it "despair"
simplified too much.
I was fighting against this simplification.
While whispering, softly, the words
"loneliness" and "despair," their imputations
began to have their effect on me,
and so the story automatically
completed itself.

物語が始まって、
ひとりでにその物語が、
終わっていくのだった。
クリティカル・エイジ、危機の年
私は夢を見なくなったから、
かわりに夢を生きてみる
孤独でさえなかった。
そうしたことに向こうに
本当の高原が広がっていった。

In this critical age, the year of crisis,
I slept without dreaming;
instead, I tried to live my dreams.
I wasn't even lonely.
Beyond such matters,
the true plateau stretches out.

水の否決

黄昏には吐息でしか触れえぬような
かすかな響きがある
数十年、その響きを訪ね歩いていると
土地という土地が
どのていどの水を含んでいるものなのか
足裏から伝わってくるようになるのだが
だとしたら川岸が
こんなにも乾いているのは
なぜなのだろう―

水に拒否されているもの、
川に否決されるとき
生涯というものは懶く
瞬けば余生が始まっている
とどこおるように
かえりみるように
ふるさとに包まれて
なのに起源からは隔てられるようにして。
そんなときだ、
たとえば、「祖国」という言葉のように
名指しえぬ感情が生まれるのは。
たとえば、そんなときだ
人が川の源を見たいと思うのは。
会話が交わされるたびに
存在は少しずつおびやかされるから
ときとして自分の声が聞こえなくなる
ところが川を渡るとき
見慣れた景色もしずかに揺らぎ

REJECTED BY WATER

At dusk.
The subtle vibrations only your breath registers.
Seeking such vibrations
for these last decades,
you come to know, from the soles of your feet upward,
	how much moisture
the soil of each place holds.
But why are riverbanks so dry?
Being rejected by water,
being rejected by the river,
you idle away your life,
and in the blink of an eye
you've already arrived into your late years.
Thinking that you're remaining in place,
and reflecting on yourself
in your own native land,
you stay removed from your own origin.
In such moments,
	the emotion you associate with "my native country"
is born without a referent.
In such moments,
people like to see headwaters.
Every time some casual conversation takes place,
your existence is jeopardized,
you won't be able, from time to time, to hear your own voices.
When you cross a river,
everyday scenery blurs out,
though sometimes you manage to see
yourself.

ときに、人は、
自らと出会う。

人々はその川は世界の中心に始まると信じていた。

伝承は伝える、
ユーラシア大陸に宇宙の中心があり
巨大な魚に支えられ、紺碧の空に聳え立つ、と。
そこは標高六六五六メートルの永久凍土
山裾には、天地創造神の心を映す
聖なる湖、マナサロワールが霊気をたたえる
氷雪に象られた聖山カイラス。
かたわらでは一頭の獅子が
日夜、水を噴き出し
褐色に湧き立つ四つの大河が生まれる
名づければ、
獅泉河、牛泉河、象泉河、馬泉河、と。
一九〇七年、
スウェン・ヘディンは川の始まりをたずねた
チャンタン高原での死の彷徨のはてに。
「一人の老いた巡礼者が、二つの岩の間に
死んで横たわっていた。
彼はこの神の山をめぐる
巡礼を成し遂げるだけの体力がなかったのだ」
その魂は、老人がそう信じたように
輪廻の大会に浮き沈みしているのだろうか？
カイラスに倒れ、鳥葬に付された骨は
聖山の氷片のように見え、
大河はその下流で
少女の屍体をも流し去っていく、という。

People believe the river's source is the omphalos of the world.

Legend has it,
there's a column at the center of Eurasia
rising into the azure sky, supported by a huge fish.
That summit, at an altitude of 6,656 meters, endures frost year-round,
and on the mountain's skirt, holy Lake Manasarovar
is surrounded by an ethereal atmosphere
reflecting the will of the gods.
The shape of holy Mount Kailash is limned with ice.
Beside it, a lion spouts water night and day,
birthing the four great distinct muddy rivers.
Let's name them:
the Indus, the Ganges, the Sutlej, the Yarlung Zangbo.
In 1907,
Sven Hedin visited the source of these rivers
after his deadly journey to the highland of Qiangtang.
"An aged pilgrim lay dead
between two blocks of stone.
He did not have the strength
to finish the pilgrimage around the divine mountain."
Is his soul now drifting over or under what he believed
was the sea of reincarnation?
The bones laid out at the foot of the Kailash
and left for sky burial look
like shards of ice strewn across the holy mountain,
and a young girl can lose her life and be washed away
        even from the mouth of a river.

漂鳥

私のなかの千の国—
その奥底にさらに何かがわだかまる
ことごとくは　心象なのか
心象があふれて言葉と化した
荒野にすぎないのか
身の老い鎮まっていくときにだけ
聞こえてくる音がある
けれども、それを
音と呼んでもいいものか
どのような震えでもなくて
むしろ　何かの香りのようなのだ
人が死に
人が死ぬように死者も死に
さらに二度死んだ者は三度死に
「死後」を満たしていくようなのだ
このように水に恵まれた邦にあっては
人の生死もさだかではなくて。

ふと、雪の匂いがした。

次第に蒼ざめていく余白で
まだ一行目が記されていない余白の
空が堕落する
　（それから五百年は過ぎ）
まだ書かれていない二行目で
水鶏が鳴き始める
その声が空と混じるあたりから
　（さらに三百年が過ぎ）

66

from The Illusory Mother (2010)

WANDERING BIRDS

A thousand countries in myself—
There's something that precipitates to the very bottom of such a feeling.
Is everything just an image,
or is this only a wasteland where images overflow
and become a language?
There is a sound you can hear
only when your body grows older and more tranquil.
And yet, can it be called "a sound"?
It's more a smell
than a sound.
People die,
just as the dead die,
and then those who died twice
die three times,
and they seem to fill "afterdeath."
As such, in regions where water is abundant,
human life and death aren't separated out.

Odor of snow.

In the margin, going paler and paler,
where not even one line has been written,
an empty sky has already collapsed.
(After that, 500 years pass.)
And in the second line, not yet written,
a water rail begins to chirp.
Where the chirp merges with the sky
(another 300 years pass)
a river begins,

川は始まるのだろう
神々さえ供物にして。
滞（とどこお）るように　立ち止まるように
顧（かえり）みるかのように　舞うように
狂っていくように。

すでに神々も去って。

けぶれる乳房のような山々も
幽暗（おぐら）く大気に沈んでいる
山がこんなにも低いので
雲は犬の舌のように立ちこめ
空があまりに低いので
川はいよいよ凍え
手を差し入れるなら
流れはふたつに分かれて
生死のように
さらに澄み渡っていくだろう

このあたりでは
樹々の名をたずねても
「あれは、樹」という応（こた）えが返ってくるだけなのだ
そう、あれは樹。
そう、あれは山。
そう、そして、これは水。
「この土地では
人よりの狐狸の類（たぐい）のほうが多い
人だと思っても
それは人ではない
毛物（けもの）が化けているか
それともどこかが透けていたら
昔、人だったものだ」
そう、あれは人？

68

offering the gods an entrance,
as if remaining in place;
      you stop where you are,
      reflecting on yourself,
      dancing,
      going mad.

And the gods are already gone.

The breastlike mountains
sink below the misty, gloomy air.
The mountains are so low,
clouds, like a dog's tongue, lap at them.
The skies are so low,
the river gets much colder.
Sticking your hand into the flow
you cleave the stream into two
currents that come clear as life and death.

Around here,
when you ask the name of a tree,
what you'll hear is, "It's a tree."
Yes, that's a tree.
Yes, that's a mountain.
Yes, and this is water.
"Here in this place,
there are more badgers and foxes than people.
You may see a human
who is not human,
who is some hirsute creature
disguised,
and if you see some part of its body
is transparent,
you'll know for sure it once was human."

何やら、生きている人がなつかしい

私のなかの千の国—
どこからともなく現われて
何も語らぬのが、父。
気づくと枕元に膝を折り
ほほえんでいるのが、母。
うっすらと痛みを曳いて
夜ごとの幻は通り過ぎ
漂鳥は渡りを見送って、
かなしい声で啼くだろう。
その声は雲を呼び、
明日はきっと雪になる。

Well, is that a human?

It may be I miss the living.

The thousand countries within me—
appearing from nowhere
and uttering nothing: this is my father.
Sitting upright with her legs folded
and smiling unselfconsciously,
my mother.
Every night, the illusion passes,
leaving a sliver of pain;
wandering birds chirp sadly,
not given to flying anywhere else.
The birdsong carries up to the clouds,
tomorrow it will snow.

跋

　タクラマカン砂漠に、夏の二ヶ月だけ、突然、出現する大河があるという。崑崙山脈の雪解け水が次第に集って、死の土地に忽然と姿を現し、砂漠を南北に貫いて流れる幻の大河、ホータン。それは、日本の川となんと異っていることか。

　上古の昔、孔子は川のほとりにあって「往くものはかくの如きか、昼夜を措かず」と嘆じた。この『論語』に見える一節は、休むことなく自らでありつづけるものへの感嘆であるとともに、ひたすらに過ぎていく時間の無情を嘆くものであったのだろう。

　絶え間なく流れつづけるもの。川を、人生や時間になぞらえて眺めるのは、東洋においては、むしろ、ふつうの感覚であった。

　しかし、どんな川にも始まりがあって、終わりがある。いつのころからか、私は、故郷に流れる北上川を河口から歩き始めて、その源流を訪ねてみたいと思うようになった。

　その川の名は、日本の神話的な時代に、大和から「まつろわぬ民」とされた、もうひとつの国、「日高見」に由来している。しかも「北上」という名をもちながら、その川はひたすら南下するだけなのだ。だからこそ、私は北上して、川の始まりを見たいと考えるようになったのかもしれない。

　源流を訪ねる旅となると、スウェン・ヘディンのことが思い浮かぶ。さまよえる湖、ロプ・ノールを発見したその探検家は、一九〇七年に、ヒマラヤ山脈の北に聳える独立峰、カイラスへと旅をした。カイラスは仏教徒、ヒンドゥー教徒、ジャイナ教徒、ボン教徒にとって、い

72

AFTERWORD

In the Taklamakan Desert, they say, there appears suddenly, only in summer for two months, a great river. The melting snow from the Kunlun Mountains gradually gathers into a river that rushes through the desert from south to north. The Hotan River. How different from the rivers in Japan.

Once upon a time, Confucius, looking at a river from the bank, grieved that life "is what passes like that, indeed, not stopping day, night" (*Confucian Analects* 9.16, translated by Ezra Pound). The meaning of this sentence must combine the admiration for what continuously stays the same with the sorrow for time's merciless passing.

A river that continuously flows. The ordinary Eastern cast of mind might compare a river to life or to time, and so deepen its resonance.

But any river has its beginning and its end. I don't remember when I began to conceive of walking from the mouth to the head of the Kitakami River, which flows through my homeland.

The river's name derives from a word, *Hitakami,* used to describe ancient Japan, whose capital, Yamato (Nara), meant "a disobedient people." And though the river's kanji can be read as "going up to the north," that river in fact flows straight south. Which may be one of the reasons I wanted to see its source.

As for visiting the head of a river, the name Sven Hedin comes to mind. This explorer who found Lake Lob-nor, "the Wandering Lake," launched an expedition to Mount Kailash, north of the Himalayan Range, in 1907. Even still, Mount Kailash is the most sacred place for Buddhists, Hindus, Jains, and Bonpos, and this unclimbed peak and its area create the head of the four great rivers.

Having Hedin's book in my bag, I began my own travel, and this book of poems can also be read as a record of that travel. What was it that the concept "river's source" taught me? Now thinking back on

まだに最高の聖地とされる場所であり、その未踏峰の聖域は、インダス河、ガンジス河など四つの大河の源流とされている。

　スウェン・ヘディンの記録を鞄に、私も旅を始めたのだが、本書は、その幻の旅誌でもある。はたして、川の始まりは、私に何を教えたのか。おそらく、それは、人生や時間の比喩として語りうるものではなかったのだと、今にして思う。

二〇一〇年二月十五日

what it meant to me, perhaps I'd say it wasn't something that can be talked through as a metaphor of life or time.

February 15, 2010

夏の錬金術

夏が来たならば
　　　　　　　ひたすら雲を観察し
とどまることのないその“変 化”を記録する
その背景には、
　　　　　　　　人の心よりも陰影に満ちた
　　　　　　　　　　　　　　　　　　（青空）
果て知らぬ広がりにさえ
　　　　　　　　　　“情動”があるとしたら
地上の生命はみな泣き濡れるだろう
草原の国から来た人は
海を前にして立ちつくす
もし、嘆き悲しむのなら
　　　　　　　　　　　声が尽きるまで。
そして、響きが消え失せるとき
　　　　　　　　　　　　そこに「存在」はない
深く夢見るように
　　　　　　　　緑の野に沈み
“好物”の臭跡をたどる
　　　　　　　　　　小動物には
尋常ではない＜危機＞が迫っている
その遠近法からは
「悪意」のスレートは滑り落ち
食うものは、ときには
食われるものであるという
地上の構図が浮かび上がってくるだろう
　　　　　　　　　　　　　　人間もまた、
虎に喰われるほど自由だ、
「聖典」を求めて旅した

ALCHEMY OF SUMMER

When summer comes,
          I just keep observing clouds
and recording their endlessly changing "nuances."
(The blue sky)
          is behind them, with much subtler nuances
                    than human minds.
If this infinite expanse
          could express its own emotions,
the faces of all living things on this earth would be covered with tears.
He who came from the desert country
stands motionless before the sea.
If you have to wail,
          wail until your voice is lost.
And when your wail stops resounding,
                    there will be no such thing as "existence."
For those small animals—
          following the spoor of their "favorite games,"
lurking in the green field
          as if sinking deep into their dreams—
"extreme dangers" approach.
From their perspectives,
"malice" swoops down from above,
although sometimes those who do the devouring
get devoured.
So the laws of nature surface.
          Human beings
are free to let themselves be devoured by a tiger
like that ancient prince
          on his quest for sutras.

　　　　　　古の皇子のように。
山林ばかりの国なのに
　　　　　　　　＜農耕民族＞は
誰もが平らなところに住もうとする
山々は、神々の座所、
　　　　　　　　　呪言神も住まうので
肉体を持って近づいてはならない
自分の影を踏むように右往左往する人々に
（太陽）よりも眩しい天体で
　　　　　　　　　　　　＜水＞が発見されたという
　　　ニュースが届く日、
湧き立つ雲を金色の階梯に染めながら
昇ってくる、夏。
その比類ない錬金術は
地にある者に＜沈黙＞を教えるだろう。

In this land of forests and mountains,
                    these "agricultural people"
choose to live on the plains.
Mountains are where gods,
                    even gods who cast evil spells, are seated—
you're not supposed to physically approach them.
On the day the news reveals that water was found
                              on some celestial body,
while people hustle and bustle trying not to step on their own shadows,
summer rises up, turning the billowing clouds
into a golden ladder.
This extraordinary alchemical event will introduce
"silence" to the people on Earth.

小さな数式

（夕焼け）は、
　　　　　　　誰にとって"赤い"のか？
人間の目には
　　　　　　大気に散乱する
　　　　　　　　　　　赤の波長が届くが
紫外線まで視える鳥たちにとっては
夕焼けとは、もっと蒼ざめたもの。
そして、地上に生命という生命が絶えたとき
あらゆる色彩は
　　　　　　「存在」しなくなる
夏至を過ぎると。
海には稠密な雲が積み上がり
何かに誘われているような気がして
子供たちは落ち着かなくなる
そんなときには「本」なんか読めない
海や川で水神と戯れるように
しぶきを上げては
なめらかな肌にまとわりつく（水滴）に
世界を映し取る
その光学的遊戯のうちに
　　　　　　　　　　夏は過ぎ
気がつくと、何人かは
水神とともにどこかへ行ってしまって
二度と帰ってこない
残された教科書は開かれることなく
小さな数式などを隠しつづけるのだろう

A TINY LITTLE EQUATION

For whom is (the evening glow)
          "red"?
To human eyes,
      the red wavelength shimmering in the air
                  is reflected,
but to the eyes of birds
which recognize even ultraviolet rays,
the evening glow looks much paler.
And when all the lives on Earth are finally snuffed out,
and the human solstice has passed,
every color will cease to "exist."
As clouds pile up densely above the sea,
kids get restless
feeling some sort of invitation.
On such occasions, when you're unable to read a "book"
while splashing around in the sea or river
as though dancing with water gods,
you'll notice beads of water on your skin
reflecting the world.
In such an optical play,
        the summer vanishes;
some people have gone off
with the water gods
and have never come back.
Textbooks, left on a desk unopened,
hold on to their tiny equations.

（夕焼け）は、
　　　　　　誰にとって"赤い"のか？
たとえ生命という生命が絶え、
見る人がひとりもいなかったとしても。

When each and every living thing has lost its life
and there remains not a single being,
for whom is (the evening glow)
                    "red"?

壊れた光

およそ、始まりは
　　　　　　　　　"火"に包まれている
冴え渡る、
　　　　　「喜びのコラール」のように。
空はいまだに、
謎が謎に見えないほど広やかで
だから、人はそこに"謎"を探したりする
雲はなぜ白いのか
　　　　　　　　　空はなぜ青いのか
海退の痕をとどめる山脈にも
かつての海棲生物の末裔は潜み
雲に鳴き、空に吠えたりするのだが
山肌を震わす声は
　　　　　　　　　決して至りえぬ場所への＜憧憬＞にも
聞こえる
光がもたらすのが＜色彩＞
しかし、それは物理的なものではなく
　　　　　　　　　　　心理的なもの
ある種の「惑い」なのだろうか、
　　　　　　　　　　決して満たされない
　　　"恋情"のように。
（太陽）の白色光は
　　　　　　　　（地球）を美しく染め上げる
けれども光は色ではなく
色とは物象の属性でもなく
事物が反射した光の波長にほかならない
ならば、人が見る色彩とは、
　　　　　　　　　ある事物が拒否した波長、

THE REJECTED LIGHT

Essentially, the beginnings take place
                in the midst of "fire"
like the crystal-clear "Ode to Joy."
The sky goes on forever,
but a mystery doesn't always look like a mystery,
so people try to pin their mysteries to the sky:
"Why are clouds white?"
            "Why is the sky blue?"
On the ranges of mountains scored with grooves from a receding sea,
the descendants of marine forms lurk;
they cry to the clouds and howl at the sky;
their voices, which carom between mountains' steep scarps,
            sound like the "yearning" for some unreachable place.
The light lets "colors" exist,
but those colors don't exist physically
            so much as they exist psychologically.
Or are they some kind of "indecision,"
            something like "a nascent feeling" never to be filled out?
The white light from "the sun"
            slaps colors against "the earth."
But light has no color
since color isn't an attribute of anything
but only the visible wavelength reflected from a thing.
Accordingly, the wavelengths people see
            are those rejected by things.
So, color: "a rejected tatter of light."
In such a place as this,
is it possible

すなわち「壊れた光」にほかならない。
そこから、
　　　　愛と憎しみについて、
　　　　語ることができるだろうか？
太陽光が「興奮」するとき、
地球を戴冠させる
　　　　　　　（曙の女神）。
およそ、始まりは"火"に包まれ、
揺らぐ北極光のなかで
　　　　　　　　世界は海のようだ。

to talk about love
and hate?

When the sun rays "get excited,"
Aurora, goddess of the dawn, crowns the earth.
Essentially, the beginnings take place in the midst of "fire,"
surrounded by the waving northern lights—

                     our whole world seems like the sea.

CODA

序―祭文

転喩の破綻ではないか　さらなる愚行を前にして「唯一」が世界に散逸し名残の境神（さかえのかみ）が朽ちている　悲しむな、悲しむな、似た色などない冷たい色素で今は自分のものでもない領土を見渡して。　焦げた葉　苦い草　ここでこうして光のなかにある異教徒の相貌　フラヴィウス、クラディウス、ユリアヌス、（誰でも構いはしない（し））小説という凶器も及びはしない　（絵画を纏う、）歯と歯の間で「隻手の音声」を試み　表記の「石」をうつ　脱げ　（あるいは）耳、長くなれ　（朽ちよ）あんよはじょうず、あんよはじょうず、あんよは………　こうして長い恢復期だけが静かに始まる―悲しむな、悲しむな　時に人は隕石に撃たれて死にもするのだから　もう何も、と「召喚」は書き継がれるのだ　死者よ、とどまれ。

GRACE BEFORE SONG

To break the yoke of metaphor? And so, right there, triggering a cycle of imbecilities. "All as One"—a wave of sameness—washing out the world while the last remnants of Sakae-no-Kami (the Gods of Borders)—desiccate. Don't lament though, don't lament as you absorb this cold unsentimental view of a world that isn't ours. Scorched leaves, bitter weeds   the heathens' faces visible in the half-light.   And here are Flavius, Claudius, and Julianus (whoever they are (and))   the novel, that loaded weapon which fires only blanks while you (as though in an ink painting) try to grasp "the sound of one hand clapping"—but between your teeth! And now you take the symbolic "stone"—inscribed with words—and heave it away   (which is to say . . .): Hey, ears: time to grow out and listen up!   (Decay.) Time for us to take to our feet, to get going, take to your feet, get going, shuffle around . . .   and only then can the long recovery start—   Don't lament, don't lament   for others have been knocked dead by a shooting star.   Enough. That's how *Cité* (what is cited) must be written. What remains? Only you, the dead.

"Wandering Beyond": The poem title comes from the first chapter of the *Chuang Tzu*.

In Buddhism, piling up round pebbles is an impossible act, which those who precede their parents in death perform after leaving this world.

"The Title Lost": The Emperor Kotoku issued laws in AD 646, after the reformation in the same year. Among them was the provision in the poem, "Set borders over mountains and rivers."

Fossa Magna is the rift valley that lies between East and West Japan.

"Rejected by Water": "An aged pilgrim lay dead . . . " is quoted from *A Conquest of Tibet,* by Sven Hedin.

"Alchemy of Summer": The "ancient prince" is the main character in the novel *Takaoka Shinno Kokai-ki* (The Voyages of Prince Takaoka), by Tatsuhiko Shibusawa. In this novel, the prince heads for India, but after going through many hardships, he falls ill. He comes up with a plan to let a tiger devour him, trusting that the tiger at least will eventually get to India. And so the prince reaches his destination reincarnated as the tiger.

"Grace before Song": This last poem is actually the earliest (circa 1985) of the poems in this collection, a signal poem for Kido; with it, he abandoned an older style and inaugurated a new one. *In the end is my beginning . . .*

ABOUT THE AUTHOR

Shuri Kido, known familiarly as "the far north poet," is considered one of the most influential contemporary poets in Japan. He has published many books of poetry and essays, and introduced to Japan translations of works by Ezra Pound and T.S. Eliot. His work is infused with a profound knowledge of Japanese culture.

ABOUT THE TRANSLATORS

Tomoyuki Endo is an assistant professor at Wako University in Tokyo, focusing on modernists and postmodernists such as Ezra Pound, William Carlos Williams, T.S. Eliot, Gary Snyder, Allen Ginsberg, Junzaburo Nishiwaki, Katue Kitasono, and Kazuko Shiraishi, along with literary pop artists including Bob Marley, Bob Dylan, and Bruce Springsteen. He has collaborated with Forrest Gander on the translation of three poems from Shiraishi's *My Floating Mother, City* (New Directions). He also served as supervisor of English subtitles for Gozo Yoshimasu's award-winning films *Thousands of Islands* and *The Reality behind What We See.*

Forrest Gander, born in the Mojave Desert, lives in California. A translator and multiple-genre writer with degrees in geology and literature, he's the recipient of numerous awards, among them the Pulitzer Prize and the Best Translated Book Award, and fellowships from the Library of Congress, the Guggenheim Foundation, and United States Artists Foundation.

Poetry is vital to language and living. Since 1972, Copper Canyon Press has published extraordinary poetry from around the world to engage the imaginations and intellects of readers, writers, booksellers, librarians, teachers, students, and donors.

 Copper Canyon Press is grateful to the Witter Bynner Foundation for Poetry for its support of this project.

COPPER CANYON PRESS WISHES TO EXTEND A SPECIAL THANKS TO THE FOLLOWING SUPPORTERS WHO PROVIDED FUNDING DURING THE COVID-19 PANDEMIC:

4Culture
Academy of American Poets (Literary Relief Fund)
City of Seattle Office of Arts & Culture
Community of Literary Magazines and Presses (Literary Relief Fund)
Economic Development Council of Jefferson County
National Book Foundation (Literary Relief Fund)
Poetry Foundation
U.S. Department of the Treasury Payroll Protection Program

WE ARE GRATEFUL FOR THE MAJOR SUPPORT PROVIDED BY:

 academy of american poets

THE PAUL G. ALLEN FAMILY FOUNDATION

amazon literary partnership

 the point envision-enact-evolve

 OFFICE OF ARTS & CULTURE SEATTLE

 4 CULTURE

  National Endowment for the Arts ART WORKS.

 WASHINGTON STATE ARTS COMMISSION

The Chinese character for poetry is made up of two parts:
"word" and "temple." It also serves as pressmark for
Copper Canyon Press.

The poems are set in MS Mincho and Adobe Garamond Pro.
Book design and composition by Phil Kovacevich.